The Fabulous Fannie Farmer

Kitchen Scientist and America's Cook

Emma Bland Smith
Pictures by Susan Reagan

CALKINS CREEK

AN IMPRINT OF ASTRA BOOKS FOR YOUNG READERS

New York

In a house near Boston in the late 1800s, Fannie Farmer sat at the kitchen table, swinging her legs and peeling potatoes.

Or so we can imagine.

Like many girls across America, Fannie likely grew up learning to cook from her mother, making dishes that had been passed down for generations.

Now, back in the old days, recipes were different from today. Both in books and out loud, the instructions were often cloudier than clam chowder, and the measurements could be downright silly!

"a suspicion of nutmeg"

"sugar to your taste"

"as many yolks of eggs as may be necessary"

"yeast sufficient to make them light"

"a good lump of dripping or butter"

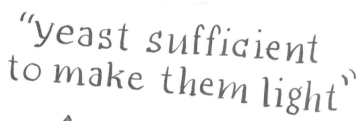

If Fannie had asked, "How much salt should I put in this soup?" her mother might have answered, "Oh, a goodly amount."

The reply to "And how much butter?" might have been "The size of a chicken's egg."

"How long should I cook it?"

"Why, till it's done, of course!"

Women weren't supposed to need exact measurements and instructions—cooking was all about feminine instincts, after all!

"I enjoy nothing so much as Cooking."

Subject
Science
- Ratio
- Reaction
- measurement

Fannie became a good cook. She loved cooking, but she never thought it could be a career. She had bigger plans. She was going to attend college, and probably become a teacher—but . . .

. . . at age sixteen, she came down with polio and lost the use of one of her legs. For several years she lay in bed. Forget finishing high school. Forget becoming a teacher.

When she did begin to walk again, it was with a strong limp. But Fannie was determined. Eager to be active and use her brain, she started cooking in her mother's kitchen, then at the home of a neighboring family. Her passion for cooking and baking rose up like a seven-layer cake!

As Fannie whipped and simmered, something revolutionary was cooking in her head. Fannie, you see, had the mind of a scientist. Through trial and error, she noticed that precise measurements made a whole heap of difference. Standard measuring cups and spoons had been invented, but few people thought they were necessary. I mean, who needs standard measurements when you've got your trusty feminine instincts, right?

"Correct measurements are absolutely necessary to insure the best results."

Fannie's family and friends urged her to enroll in the Boston Cooking School. At the age of thirty-one, she did.

(Let us take a moment to be grateful. If she hadn't enrolled, we might all still be tossing in carefree pinches of baking powder and crossing our fingers that our Boston cream pie wouldn't come out flat as a pancake.)

Fannie was a top-notch student. After she graduated, she was invited to stay on—first as an assistant, then as the principal. Fannie was going to teach!

"Cookery becomes an art rather than mere drudgery in the hands of the interested housekeeper."

Most people back then looked down on home cooking—generally the only kind women did. (Restaurant cooking was considered *very important* and *only for men*.)

But Fannie thought cooking for a family was serious business. It involved planning and budgeting, health and nutrition.

And it deserved more than terms like "a goodly amount" and "the size of an egg." Because, honestly, how else could you insure a recipe would come out the same each time?

Fannie taught her students to be precise and thoughtful, like kitchen scientists. She taught them . . .

to level off the sugar rather than heaping it,

that adding sugar to yeast would hasten fermentation,

to roll the pastry away from them to prevent breaking air bubbles,

that the acid in tomatoes tenderized the meat,
to keep the fat at a consistent temperature while frying.

A pharmacist wouldn't just toss in ingredients haphazardly
and hope for the best, so why should a cook?

"Miss F. says if a cook can make a good cream cake, baking-powder biscuits, & creamed cod fish, she can cook almost anything."

— One of Fannie's students

Women loved Fannie's can-do attitude. They packed her classes! The cooking school did so well, new teachers were hired—and Fannie made sure each one of them shared her enthusiasm and belief in science.

But there was one more thing Fannie just had to do.

"Our instructors Love their work and go into it with the same enthusiasm as if it was music or art."

The school cookbook was written in the old, murky way. Fannie decided to rewrite it.

She obsessively tested every recipe. Her students helped too, and the school's kitchen became a chemistry lab! Her recipes instructed readers how to do the most basic actions, even stirring.

"To stir, mix by using circular motion, widening the circles until all is blended."

Fannie wanted to make sure that anyone could master cooking. You didn't need luck. You didn't need expensive classes. And you certainly didn't need magical feminine instincts!

Normally confident, Fannie worried.

Would people really like her book?

The publisher she approached had doubts. They could publish the book, but they didn't want to pay for the printing. Fannie would have to cover that herself.

Did Fannie slink home in embarrassment?

I think you know the answer!

The Boston Cooking-School Cook Book

Fannie Merritt Farmer

"At the earnest solicitation of educators, pupils, and friends, I have been urged to prepare this book, and I trust it may be a help to many who need its aid."

Fannie agreed to pay—IF she could get most of the profits. (Her business savvy was as sharp as a carving knife!) Fine, said the publisher, who didn't think the book would make much money anyway.

Well, Fannie's strategy was a recipe for success. Her book was a hit—not just with students, but with home cooks all over the country! People liked that with Fannie at their side, they could make impeccable popovers and melt-in-your-mouth angel food cake. No guessing, no luck required.

Fannie's Recipes Adapted for the Modern Chef

Please ask an adult to help you with the recipes.

POPOVERS

Notes and tips:

The perfect popover rises high above the pan and is crispy outside but custardy and hollow inside.

Popovers are finicky; to get best results, follow instructions exactly.

Recipe makes six if using a specialized popover pan, and eight if using a standard muffin tin.

Prep time: 10 minutes
Bake time: 30–35 minutes

3 eggs, at room temperature or warmed in a bowl of warm water

1¼ cups milk, at room temperature or warmed 30 seconds in microwave

1 tablespoon melted butter

1¼ cups flour

½ teaspoon salt

Put pan in oven (in lower third) and preheat to 450°F.

While oven is preheating, in large bowl, whisk eggs, milk, and all but one teaspoon of melted butter until smooth, about one minute. Add flour and salt and mix vigorously until combined and all lumps are gone.

When oven is preheated, remove pan and brush insides of cups with remaining teaspoon of melted butter.

Spoon or ladle batter into cups, filling each about ½ to ¾ full.

Bake for 20 minutes (do not open oven during this first stage), then reduce heat to 350°F and bake 10–15 minutes more, or until brown.

Remove pan from the oven and turn out the popovers onto a cooling rack or plate.

Serving suggestions: Popovers are best eaten while warm. Serve for breakfast with jam, honey, or butter, for lunch with a salad, or for dinner with soup or stew.

ANGEL FOOD CAKE

Notes and tips:

Do not grease the pan, or the batter will not be able to climb the sides.

You can use a 10-inch tube pan or a specialized angel food cake pan with removable bottom.

Prep time: 15 minutes
Bake time: 45 minutes

10 egg whites, at room temperature
1 teaspoon cream of tartar
¼ teaspoon salt
¼ teaspoon almond extract (optional)
1 teaspoon vanilla extract
1¼ cups sugar
1 cup cake flour

Preheat oven to 325°F.

With hand or stand mixer, beat egg whites and cream of tartar until foamy. Add salt and continue beating until soft peaks form.

Mix in almond and vanilla extracts and beat until stiff peaks form.

As mixer runs on lowest setting, gradually mix in sugar.

Gradually sift flour over batter and fold in by hand with rubber spatula. (Do not beat or batter will deflate.)

Pour batter into ungreased pan.

Bake for 45 minutes or until top is light brown.

Remove pan from the oven.

Turn upside down onto rack and let cool in pan. Carefully loosen cake with knife, and turn out onto plate.

Serving suggestions: Slice the cake with serrated knife and top with homemade whipped cream and berries, or spread with buttercream frosting, or drizzle with chocolate sauce.

Everyone loved Fannie's book. But this revolutionary lady wasn't yet ready to set down her measuring spoons. She started her own cooking school, lectured all over the country, and even taught at Harvard Medical School! Fannie kept on cooking for the rest of her life. And those of us who appreciate a perfect pie or delectable doughnut salute her, our mouths and tummies full.

Educational

Miss Farmer's SCHOOL -OF- COOKERY

30 HUNTINGTON AVENUE
BOSTON, MASS

— **SUMMER COURSE** —

-Y 7 to AUGUST 11, 1908

Two sessions each week-day, Saturdays excepted

OUTLINE OF WORK

tical Dietetics
2 lectures

Sewing
2 classes weekly
2 hours each
employed

nt and Child F
2 classes

d Organic C
lectures

Cookery
ectures

in Kitch

a Wai
actices

3 w

POSTCARD

"I am working to my limit and I am surprised at myself."
Fannie

BALTIMORE & OHIO R.R.CO.

13678

DETROIT, MICH

Good for one passage

Fare $ 1.95

Union Pacific

TRACK NUMBER 142
DESTINATION
FROM: Boston
TO: St Louis
Departure time   arrival time

Ticket # E 9600

SEAL OF THE STATE OF ILLINOIS
AUG. 26. 1818

TIMES SQUARE
HOTEL   RESTAURANT
1000 ROOMS   RADIO IN EVERY ROOM
NEW YORK

HOTEL SUISSE
LUCERNE
MONTANA

CONTINENTAL
HOTEL

APPLE PIE

6 to 8 sour apples
½ to ¾ cup sugar, white or brown
¼ teaspoon grated nutmeg or cinnamon

¼ teaspoon s...
½ tablespoon...
...teaspoons lemon juice
...few gratings lemon rind

Line pie plate with pastry. Pare, core, and cut apples in eighths, put row around plate ½ inch from ed... and work towards center until plate is covered; then pile on remainder. Mix sugar, nutme... salt, lemon juice, and grated rind, and sprinkle over apples, ... over with butter. We... of undercrust, cover with upper ... and press edges tog... ...e several places with fork. ... Evaporated apples... ...cold water, may be place of fresh...

...Mix sugar, nutmeg, salt, lemon juice, and grated rind...

...work toward the center until plate is covered...

...AIN PASTRY

⅓ cup lard or vegeta... shortening
Ice water (abou...
...butter and la...
...shortening is...
...x and m...
...xed pa...

A Note About Research, Fiction, and Nonfiction

Because Fannie Farmer grew up so long ago, and because she wasn't famous as a child or young woman, there is almost no recorded information about her early years. We know when and where she was born. We know some basic facts about her parents and siblings. And very occasionally, in her columns, Fannie dropped an anecdote about her childhood or personal life.

In order to bring Fannie to life, I imagined certain scenes—but in the text I make clear that these are indeed imagined and not based on fact. For example, we don't know for sure that Fannie helped her mother peel potatoes (although it is very likely), so I added the line "or so we can imagine."

Being clear about the distinction between facts and imagined scenes, between fiction and nonfiction, is crucial.

Boston Cooking School students came from all walks of life. There were housewives, servants sent at their employers' expense, and young women hoping to become cooking instructors themselves.

Fannie's Legacy

Like many people, I have my own well-worn copy of Fannie Farmer's cookbook. Mine was gifted to me by my grandmother when I was twenty-four years old and just beginning to cook seriously. My copy is old: It was published in 1944. But that is young by the standards of this remarkable book. Still in print after well over a century, Fannie's cookbook has sold more than seven million copies! What makes it so popular?

Some might think Fannie Farmer was an advertising invention, a fake, a figurehead—such as the completely invented Betty Crocker. But Fannie was a real person,

and the story behind her cookbook is a fascinating and inspiring one.

The first Fannie Farmer cookbook, from 1896, was actually titled *The Boston Cooking-School Cook Book*. (It was an update of an existing book written by the school's previous director, Mary Lincoln.) It became an immediate success!

In 1896, there were few published cookbooks, and even fewer with the appeal of Fannie's. Fannie revolutionized home cooking. By bringing straightforward, comprehensive instructions and cutting-edge scientific strategies to the field, she helped make excellent home cooking accessible to everyone.

Today, we still use the measurements Fannie pioneered—standard measuring cups, tablespoons, and teaspoons. Fannie specified exactly how big or small to chop vegetables, and occasionally went so far as to specify how many grains of spices to use in a dish. She explained in a matter-of-fact style why ingredients reacted a certain way and how to manipulate them to get the desired result. Her ultimate goal was to give women the confidence to produce a delicious, attractive meal without relying on luck or guesswork.

Fannie was known for testing recipes as many times as necessary to get every aspect perfect. Even after her students produced a perfect dish, she would ask,

Fannie (at center with glasses) poses surrounded by the Boston Cooking School graduating class of 1900. Fannie was an energetic, enthusiastic teacher, much liked and respected by students and colleagues alike.

"Could it be bettered?" If she heard about an amazing new meal at a restaurant, she would rush out to sample it, and sometimes sneak a bit home in order to further analyze the flavors. She really was something of a kitchen scientist. (One writer referred to her ability to "Sherlock Holmes" a chef's dish—to deduce the methods and ingredients.)

She was precise, practical, and inventive, as when she instructed readers to use baking powder boxes as molds to create uniform sandwiches.

But Fannie's more playful, enthusiastic side came out in the monthly columns she wrote for the popular magazine *Woman's Home Companion*. These dishes were often fun and elaborate, with an emphasis on delicious ingredients and whimsical, even theatrical, presentation. She expected home cooking to be "as pretty as it is good." In an Easter column, she walked readers through shaping little animals from mashed potatoes. A column on fruit desserts instructed readers to carve out a homemade cake, fill it with fresh raspberries, and top it all with sweetened whipped cream. (She had a definite sweet tooth!) Fannie expressed her creativity and love for good food through these delightful articles.

Later the world came to know other great women cookbook authors and chefs, women such as Irma Rombauer, Alice Waters, Julia Child, Martha Stewart, Joyce Chen, Edna Lewis, Marcella Hazan, Ina Garten, Lidia Bastianich, and Marion Cunningham (who rewrote the Fannie Farmer cookbook in 1979). Each worked magic in the kitchen in her own personal style.

Fannie Farmer paved the way.

Fannie's Physical Condition

When she was a student at Medford High School, Fannie tried to get out of bed one morning and instead fell on the floor, one of her legs paralyzed. The doctors at the time called it infantile paralysis or a ruptured blood vessel, but today we believe she had polio. Fannie spent months unable to walk and stayed in her bed or a wheelchair for several years. She eventually did learn to walk again, although with a limp, and was a highly energetic and active person the rest of her life. In her fifties, her health declined, and for her last few years, she taught and lectured from a wheelchair.

The Mother of Measurement

"Tin measuring-cups . . . may be bought at any store where kitchen furnishings are sold."

"Good judgment, with experience, has taught some to measure by sight; but the majority need definite guides."

Fannie is sometimes credited with inventing standardized measurements such as the cup and teaspoon. (In fact, the idea for this book came to me when my daughter dressed up as Fannie Farmer for a fourth-grade unit on inventors!) In reality, she did not invent them, but she did use her position as an influential cooking figure to aggressively promote them.

This photo appeared in the April 1894 issue of the *New England Kitchen Magazine*. Classes at the Boston Cooking School ranged from single private lessons (costing $2.75), to weekly lectures, to a six-month live-in course ($125 plus $5 per month for room and board).

It is thanks to Fannie that today, recipes might call for a tablespoon of butter and not an egg-size or a walnut-size chunk! "Correct measurements are absolutely necessary to insure the best results," she wrote.

She devoted a full page in her cookbook to explaining how to measure, focusing on leveling, not heaping, the cups and spoons. In her weekly column in *Woman's Home Companion*, these lines ran under each column: "In my recipes all measurements are made level. Measuring cups divided into thirds and quarters are used, also tea and table measuring spoons."

Indeed, she commonly gave such specific and minute measurements as "one eighth of a teaspoonful of salt," "3/8 cup hot water," "a few drops of onion juice," and "few grains of cayenne"—quite a far cry from "a pinch" or "a good splash"!

The Birth of the Modern American Recipe

Before Fannie Farmer's time, most recipes were written in a narrative format with no particular structure. Often they included stories and chatty comments, and were hard to follow and read. Fannie, on the other hand, insisted on using a very specific format for her recipes: a vertical list of ingredients followed by clear instructions. Today, most cookbook writers still use the format that Fannie popularized.

The Right Moment for a New Cookbook

"Progress in civilization has been accompanied by progress in cooking."

When Fannie Farmer wrote her cookbook, the world was in the throes of an industrial revolution. An emerging interest in science and technology was changing the cultural landscape. That set the scene for the success of her methods. New instruments like standardized measuring tools and ovens with temperature gauges allowed for precision in the kitchen. People were ready for a new kind of cooking that had science behind it.

However, there were other factors that contributed to the success of Fannie's cookbook. One was the new mobility of the American population. For centuries, women had grown up learning to cook from their mothers and grandmothers. Now, it was common for young adults to leave their hometowns and settle far away, where they had no family to teach them to cook.

In addition, immigrants were arriving in large numbers in this young country. They too lacked a family close at hand to learn from. Many of these young women turned to cookbooks to master the art of cooking for their families. Fannie's cookbook was just what they needed.

From the December 1900 issue of *Good Housekeeping*, this photo shows a Black woman in the classroom. Although this particular person may have been an employee, some women of color did take Fannie's classes. In fact, one remarkable Black woman from New Orleans, Lena Richard, was a student in 1918 and went on to become a successful chef, businesswoman, and TV show host.

Hungry for More? Resources for Kids Who Like to Cook

Books

Awesome Kitchen Science Experiments for Kids: 50 STEAM Projects You Can Eat! by Megan Olivia Hall (Rockridge Press)

Bake, Make, and Learn to Cook by David Atherton and Rachel Stubbs (Candlewick Press)

The Complete Cookbook for Young Scientists by America's Test Kitchen (America's Test Kitchen)

Cooking Class Global Feast!: 44 Recipes That Celebrate the World's Cultures by Deanna F. Cook (Storey Publishing)

The Forest Feast for Kids: Colorful Vegetarian Recipes That Are Simple to Make by Erin Gleeson (Abrams Books for Young Readers)

Kid Chef Junior Bakes: My First Kids Baking Cookbook by Charity Mathews (Rockridge Press)

Kitchen Science Lab for Kids: Edible Edition by Liz Lee Heinecke (Quarry Books)

Milk Bar: Kids Only by Christina Tosi (Clarkson Potter)

Pretend Soup and Other Real Recipes: A Cookbook for You and Your Preschooler by Mollie Katzen and Ann Henderson (Tricycle Press)

The Silver Spoon for Children: Favorite Italian Recipes by Amanda Grant and Harriet Russell (Phaidon Press)

Magazine

ChopChop

TV Series

The Great British Baking Show
MasterChef Junior
My World Kitchen

Visit

Julia Child's kitchen at the National Museum of American History in Washington, DC. americanhistory.si.edu/food/Julia-childs-kitchen.

The Teaching Kitchen at the Children's Museum of Denver at Marisco Campus in Denver, Colorado. mychildsmuseum.org/exhibits/teaching-kitchen/.

Fannie's Books

1896: *The Boston Cooking-School Cook Book* (in later editions titled *The Fannie Farmer Cookbook*)

1898: *Chafing Dish Possibilities*

1904: *Food and Cookery for the Sick and Convalescent*

1905: *What to Have for Dinner: Containing Menus with Recipes for Their Preparation*

1911: *Catering for Special Occasions, with Menus and Recipes*

1912: *A New Book of Cookery: Eight Hundred and Sixty Recipes, Covering the Whole Range of Cookery*

An early edition of Fannie's cookbook, first published in 1896. In Fannie's lifetime the book sold over 300,000 copies. To date it has sold more than seven million.

Timeline

1857: Fannie Merritt Farmer is born in Boston, Massachusetts, to a printer and his wife. She later has three sisters. They grow up in Medford, a suburb of Boston. Her parents expect all their daughters to become schoolteachers. Fannie is considered especially bright, and her parents hope for her to attend college.

1873: At age sixteen, while a student at Medford High School, Fannie develops paralysis in her leg, probably due to polio. She cannot walk for several years. When she does walk again, it is with a pronounced limp. She never graduates from high school.

1888: Fannie has become an excellent cook. At the age of thirty-one, at the urging of her friends and family, who see her talent, she enrolls in the Boston Cooking School.

1889: Fannie graduates and is hired as assistant to the director.

1891: She becomes head of the school. She begins to gain success and popularity as a teacher and lecturer.

1896: Fannie rewrites and expands *The Boston Cooking-School Cook Book*, published by Little, Brown. Doubtful of its potential, the publisher prints a modest first run of three thousand copies and requires that Fannie cover the costs, in return for her getting to claim the lion's share of the profits. In her lifetime alone the book goes on to sell over three hundred thousand copies. To date it has sold over seven million copies.

1902: Fannie opens her own cooking school, Miss Farmer's School of Cookery.

1905–1915: She writes a regular weekly column for *Woman's Home Companion*, lectures in Boston and all over the United States, and even speaks to students at Harvard Medical School about diet and nutrition for convalescents.

1915: Fannie dies at age fifty-seven, on January 15, in Boston. She lectured just ten days before her death.

From the November 1901 issue of *Good Housekeeping*, Fannie (in hammock) relaxes with family at her summer home. In the article, she declared that after preparing elaborate meals for work all day long, she liked simple food at home: "I would prefer a plain, well-cooked steak to all the fancy dishes ever dreamed of." She added that in summer, she and her family ate ice cream for dessert every night.

Bibliography

*All quotations can be found in sources marked with an asterisk.**

Boston Evening Transcript. "Miss Fannie M. Farmer Dead." January 15, 1915, 1.

*Curtis, Isabel Gordon. "A Visit to the Boston Cooking School." *Good Housekeeping*, December 1900, 320–324.

*Farmer, Fannie Merritt. Monthly cooking column, 1905–1915. *Woman's Home Companion*, February 1907, February 1908, January 1909, April 1909, June 1909, January 1910.

*————. *The Boston Cooking-School Cook Book*. Boston: Little, Brown, 1896.

Good Housekeeping. "The Housekeeper at Large: The People She Meets." November 1901, 426–428.

*Hartt, Mary Bronson. "Fannie Merritt Farmer—An Appreciation." *Woman's Home Companion*, December 1915.

Kimball, Chris. *Fannie's Last Supper: Re-creating One Amazing Meal from Fannie Farmer's 1896 Cookbook*. New York: Hyperion, 2010.

Lincoln, Mary. *Mrs. Lincoln's Boston Cook Book*. Boston: Roberts Brothers, 1883.

New England Kitchen Magazine. "The Boston Cooking School," April 1894.

Perkins, Dexter. *Yield of the Years*. Boston: Little, Brown, 1969.

Perkins, Wilma Lord. Letter to Margo Miller, 1974.

*Shapiro, Laura. *Perfection Salad: Women and Cooking at the Turn of the Century*. Berkeley: University of California Press, 2001.

Smith, Andrew F. *Eating History: 30 Turning Points in the Making of American Cuisine*. New York: Columbia University Press, 2009.

Willan, Anne. *Women in the Kitchen: Twelve Essential Cookbook Writers Who Defined the Way We Eat, from 1661 to Today*. New York: Scribner, 2020.

Woman's Home Companion. "Our Own Folks." March 1914, 1.

Acknowledgments

Many thanks to Margo Miller, Erica Peters, Meg Ragland, Marcia Reed, Laura Shapiro, and Anne Willan, who all helped me immeasurably with my research. And thank you to Mandy Sather and Kimmie Wong for helping test the recipes! —EBS

Picture credits

Bettman/Contributor: 32; Collection of the Massachusetts Historical Society: 33; Schlesinger Library, Radcliffe Institute, Harvard University: 35; UC Berkeley Libraries: 36, 38; Everett Smith: 37.

To the senior women of the Bland, Smith, and Wilson clans,
who shared their kitchen wisdom with me and made me a
cook: Anne, Bobbie, Holly, Judy, Laurel, and Sally —*EBS*

For love of art and eating. The cooking I leave to Emma and Fannie —*SR*

For information about permission to reproduce selections from this book,
please contact permissions@astrapublishinghouse.com.

Calkins Creek
An imprint of Astra Books for Young Readers, a division of Astra Publishing House
astrapublishinghouse.com

Printed in China

ISBN: 978-1-63592-612-5 (hc)
ISBN: 978-1-63592-613-2 (eBook)
Library of Congress Control Number: 2023905131

First edition

10 9 8 7 6 5 4 3 2 1

Design by Barbara Grzeslo
The text is set in ITC Franklin Gothic Std.
The artwork combines traditional watercolor with digital drawing.